Care More
Than Us

The Young People's
Guide to Success

Written by

Glen Mourning

D1310847

ISBN:1532730535

ISBN-13:9781532730535

DEDICATION

In a world full of challenges, young people may have it the hardest when it comes to learning how to make the most out of life. And when you are fortunate enough to make it from childhood to adulthood, remember that along the way there were plenty of grown-ups who cared for you at times, more than you cared for yourself. This book is dedicated to all of the loving adults around the world who want the most out of life for the young people that they serve. It truly takes a village to get these kids and teenagers of ours to see their full potential. Coach Davis, thank you for all that you've done. R.I.P

CONTENTS

Special Thank You

To Herman Izzard, my mentor of twenty-five years. It is because of caring and passionate motivators in our world like you, that I am able to continue down the road of success. You have shown me how to reshape and readjust my focus to find opportunities to succeed. I thank you from the bottom of my heart for modeling how to take action, for teaching me how to take advantage of the many windows of opportunity and for encouraging me to believe.

ACKNOWLEDGMENTS

To my mother Lillian...Without your support and unconditional love, I would have truly given up on myself as a kid and as a young man. Growing up was rough and school was challenging. But when I learned how listening to your advice along with how the power of education could open the door to a better tomorrow, I was able to wake up each morning with a purpose. You made me believe in me! Thank you to all of the amazing parents, guardians, teachers, coaches and mentors around the world. Your efforts are absolutely necessary and appreciated.

THE

Introduction

Imagine what it would be like if the adults in your life cared about you more than they cared about anything else in the entire world. Now, imagine that the adults who do care for you such as parents, grandparents, aunts, uncles, coaches and especially teachers, would sacrifice anything and everything for you to have an amazing life. How would the world be if these adults were willing to do anything and everything they could if it meant that you would grow up to be as successful as possible?

Fortunately enough for you, this world that I'm speaking of already exists. All of the positive decisions and support provided by every adult in your life **correlates** with one another. Every single day of your life, you are in the company of an adult. At times it looks like relatives or guardians caring for you. This also takes place at sports practices or in after-school programs when you participate in any extracurricular activity. And for ten whole months out of the year, Monday through Friday, for about seven hours a day, these adults that I am speaking so highly of are your teachers!

At first, these teachers and adults are strangers to you. But as time goes on they become the men and women who want nothing but the absolute best for each and every one of their students. Of course some of you have your support staff at home, like your mom or dad, or maybe even a grandmother and grandfather. But for some kids, that isn't enough and that is okay.

From the very moment a teacher has the opportunity to meet you, they instantly become your biggest fans, where they immediately invest in your future. When teachers see the expressions on their student's smiling faces, the natural and genuine reaction is usually, them immediately believing in their group of kids!

Understand that when things seem too hard to do, or even impossible to finish, that if you look in the right places there will always be an adult nearby to lend you their support. These adults can't wait for opportunities to add value to your life and to show you that they absolutely believe in you!

It is true that we adults care about you more than you'll ever know. But do remember, in order for you to become the best that you can be in anything in life, there will come a time when you will need to care for your own development, your own education, and your your own future, way more than we do.

So time for a little *truth*. Teachers do not make a lot of money to do what we do when we first start off.

Becoming a teacher is a **commitment** that most people fail to understand. And parents might confess that having you as their child was the best thing to ever happen to them. But the truth is, children are a gift, but one that comes with a large price. And by price, I don't mean money…I'm talking about the price of *sacrifice.* Many adults look at their friends who are teachers or who are parents and say things like, "are you crazy? Why on earth would you want to teach kids or raise children who seem not to listen or who don't try their hardest at being their best?"

Some adults who are close friends with teachers or who are close friends with parents think that teaching or parenting is either a hard job because the students or children drive them *crazy,* or that teaching and being a parent is the easiest job in the world, kind of like sitting around all day and babysitting. Until adults experience either of the lifestyles on their own, it will remain difficult to **comprehend**. Well, life for adults that choose to teach and for adults who choose to parent is actually very challenging. However, what these friends of ours don't get to see at time is how teaching and being the primary **influence** for a child are the absolute most rewarding and enjoyable jobs in the world; when kids learn how to care more than us.

Speaking specifically about being an educator, teaching can be hard for lots of different reasons. Most teachers work very long hours and do not get paid any extra money to do so. Sometimes, teaching is extremely difficult because teachers care so much about their kids that they worry about them all day and night, even after school is over; similarly to how a parent thinks and worries all day when their children are dropped off or make it to school for the day. These instances go hand in hand and are two of the components of extremely successful communities.

But like I said earlier, because we believe in you all and because we truly know how important teaching is along with understanding the continuous effort that it takes to be a successful parent, *none of those* amazing experiences matter if we can't get you all to *believe* in yourselves in order to continue improving your own lives.

A piece of advice from a caring teacher...

Instead of saying, "I don't get it" as soon as your teacher hands out an activity, give yourself a chance to read the directions. Sometimes in life, things seem way harder than they actually are. If you believe in yourself, you will be able to surprise yourself with accomplishing something that you would have given up on.

I dare you to try your hardest. You can do it, but you have to believe you can! After you are done reading the young person's guide to success, it will be your turn to show us teachers and parents what you've got!

CHAPTER 1

The lie of all lies

Can you imagine being lied to every single day of your life? Well…maybe not every single day but perhaps several times throughout the week or month. Chances are, if you haven't been mislead on occasion, you have at least been misguided and lied to more times than you'd like to accept.

Every single child in a home, every single student in all of the classrooms around the country, throughout every city and state, as well as the millions of adults that walk our wonderful planet have been lied to. As

citizens of our great country, we have been led to believe a certain false truth that I am going to provide you with a chance of seeing as clear as day with your own two eyes.

Someone, a parent, a classmate, a neighbor and unfortunately even your own **conscious** has misled and lied to you during some part of your journey in life. No one will come right out and admit it. No one will ever warn you when the lie is getting ready to be spoken out loud. No...because see, that would be too easy. It would be too easy to catch and too easy to ignore and avoid if that was in fact how this lie is presented.

Instead, this lie sneaks into the front of every grocery store line and to the front of every bus stop, metro stop, taxi stand, lunch line and stop light in America, arriving unannounced and without the slightest unveiling of a single warning sign. Ready to take a guess at what "lie" I am referring to? Here it goes...

Millions of children, teenagers and adults suffer from hearing these three words every single day, "Its...

too…late". Millions of kids, teenagers, employees, CEO's, professionals and those figuring out what's next for them in life have all been exposed to this powerful and controlling idea that haunts our spirits with the ability of ruining our futures. This lie has been brought up in conversation and has been used to distract us from maximizing our potential.

Up until this point in my life, I had never been told by a nine-year old that it was too late to learn something, for a child...to learn how to do something. He was a fourth grader in one of my classes while teaching in Washington, D.C and he was embarrassed because of his limited writing skills. When prompted to write and complete his task, he said that he sucked at writing and that since he was *already* in the fourth grade, that it was too late for him to learn how to do it. I tried asking him who on earth had told him that and he couldn't even think of anyone in particular. It had just been **a belief that his brain came to believe.**

"I hated writing, Mr. Mourning…I didn't like it at all and I wasn't good at it", was what this little guy said just like a true angry ole' grandpa each and every day of the beginning of the 2015 school year. It took some coaching, some tough love and consistent encouragement to get him to believe in himself. I shared with him that when we effectively set goals and map out how to accomplish them, that it's never too late to start. After several conversations about achieving his goal of becoming a better writer, I was able to see and notice the drastic improvements in his attitude and in his willingness to not only try new things, but to give it his all on academic writing tasks.

When asked about "school" in general, his response was pretty refreshing to hear. It had taken him five months to buy into my system and for him to truly believe that I wanted the best for him and his family.

"Umm...tell you about school...okay. School is the one place that you can try something new and don't be afraid. And sometimes even when you are not in school, don't be afraid to try new things, even though it might be hard. Sometimes when the right teacher cares about you, and you care about them

and don't disrespect them, they will not be as hard on you. Like, you really cared about me this year, Mr. Mourning and I knew that it was for real because you came to work every day in a tie and a nice shirt and nice shoes and really tried to make sure I wrote my answers even when I knew they looked crazy".

He continued to explain, which caught me off guard due to how little he spoke when the spot light was on.

"I never had that before and sometimes, even though I had annoying friends I learned how to ignore them to get the instruction from you and to keep my focus. And I think you called me "Grandpa" this year because my attitude reminded you of an old person…like even when I did my work I still needed some help and more help, like an old person (he said laughing and smiling). If I could go into the future and really be an old man, I would tell the little me to try his hardest and when things are painful and might seem like you can't do it, keep trying and trying and never give up".

The thought that it's too late to learn something, may be because those around you seem to know how to do it already. Those feelings can come from strange places.

The *lie* has made its presence felt during thousands of unique and individual scenarios, where millions of different people, all found themselves trusting this assumption that a goal, an opportunity, a dream and most importantly a chance to learn, is too late to do. Just know that once you internalize my advice and learn how to care more than us, that the negative concept will be proven false.

CHAPTER 2

What it is

from what it isn't

From childhood, to adolescence, to marriage, to retirement and up until your last breath on this planet, there is the suggested notion that "something", absolutely achievable and **obtainable** has a definite **expiration** date.

It is important to mention that there are obvious restrictions to someone's progressive mobility in society as an independent person. There are truths about what is needed to achieve certain feats in life. In regards to some experiences, appropriate, non-negotiable and necessary timing of opportunity is a factor that remains intact for specific accomplishments.

For example, the physically restrictive and concrete opportunities are not what I am referring to in this instance. Of course it would be impossible and "too late" to become a Hall of Fame NBA Superstar if you are, I don't know...let's say an out of shape, un-athletic sixty-five year old history teacher.

However, a huge percentage of desired outcomes, real life situations and potential opportunities to improve the quality of your life are and will forever be available to you. These life-changing opportunities may offer themselves to you, but are only achievable with the appropriate, **intentional** and targeted approach to succeeding.

Rather than trying to disprove my interpretation and **analysis** of adjusting your focus on life and your desired outcomes, keep an open mind. I would suggest that if you can find a way to assume positive **intent** in my messages it will serve a far greater purpose with establishing your beliefs that hundreds of your goals and aspirations are obtainable, and will continue to be for a very long time. This will ultimately allow you to define what success looks like and feels like for yourself as you take the necessary steps to shape the positive outcomes for your future. If you haven't set these type of long term goals yet, you have a lot of time to **analyze** your strengths and weaknesses about yourself to get started.

CHAPTER 3

What is success anyway?

Success does not happen for anyone without them first experiencing frustration or doubt. To become successful, it takes time. When you first try to accomplish anything in life, if it is meaningful and important to you, there is a huge chance that you will find failure or frustration with it the very first time. When thinking back on my teaching career, not every situation or experience with students has been easy to communicate as a success or as a win for everybody.

Five years ago, before the year started I had bragged about this one particular boy from a summer school session. At the time, I had told my teacher assistant that during that past Summer, I met a third grader who was going to blow her away when the Fall arrived. Well, initially I was wrong. He talked back defiantly, he refused to do work, and he couldn't keep his mouth closed to save his life. Unfamiliar perhaps with what it was going to take to make up the gaps between his ability as a student, we just couldn't get him to fully "buy in" to our philosophy as teachers and mentors.

In order to grant this one student any access to his own education and to allow him to develop into the independent learner that we knew he was capable of becoming, it would take some serious, tough-love relationship building. Getting mom on the phone early on in the year was a no-brainer. But the delivery of the messages we wanted to communicate to her and how she would receive the updates missed each other entirely. Instead of her feeling supported and comfortable, she immediate received our news as an attack on her son who was not performing close to grade level. We wanted nothing more than to show her that we did in fact want the best for her son.

But no one said building trusting and lasting relationships was going to be easy, especially if they were going to be authentic and genuine.

So in time, we reshaped how we addressed our concerns, and encouraged her son by motivating him and providing him with a purpose for achieving in our classroom. From August to April, we struggled. We struggled to stop his tears from falling, we struggled to keep his pencil in his hand and we struggled to show him why we were so hard on him. But by the end, there was growth. The growth was limited at time, but it was present to say the least. At the close of that school year, the young man had the opportunity to sharpen his skills as he was promoted to the fifth-grade. He had to precisely and accurately assess his ability, as he learned that having a second chance to find more success happens when you don't give up on yourself.

Back when I had asked him if he thought he had

worked hard enough to make it to the next grade, I remember him dropping his head as he mentioned that he knew that he could do better and that he would be making his mom proud the next time around. Social promotion is a form of moving students along who aren't ready to do so and in this case, our scholar has so much worldly knowledge and sense of self that he couldn't even disagree with our decision as educators and professionals to keep him behind for one more year in the same grade.

I may have been premature with when it came to believing that he had the ability to blow us away with his academic ability but I was correct in the sense that his charisma and charm were magnetic and very special traits that will accompany him on a path to greatness. When asked what he was going to do differently next year he responded by saying, **"I'm gonna do better next year by trying harder on my work. I will read more books and I will try to get all of my work done"**.

Sitting respectfully and patiently with his hands

crossed in his lap, he continued.

"My favorite thing about this year was the projects we finished, the pizza parties for when we had perfect attendance and the movies we watched that had something to do with the books we read in class".

Had he given up on himself some four or five years ago when we decided to keep him back in the same grade instead of promoting him as an unprepared student, he wouldn't be a year away from graduating high school with three full athletic scholarships to choose from.

So as you can imagine, the success is buried, hidden underneath the second or third time you try to do the same task or accomplish the same goal. When you don't give up and find the courage to keep digging and give it your all one final time, success happens!

In school, success can look like getting really good grades on a test or being named Class President. To some, success is when you are able to finish an assignment that at first seemed impossible to even get started on.

Finishing your homework and getting an A+ on a math test are two different examples of being successful. And the best part about this is that teachers and other adults absolutely love it when you do either or, although accomplishing both would be amazing.

So, being a successful person looks completely different depending on the specific time of day, where you are or what it is that you are doing at that moment in life. You will have to think about everything you do in attempts to bettering yourself as a person. Then **classify** those actions and choices into two categories; positive choices that help you better yourself or negative choices that take away from your potential.

When you find moments where you are successful, it is very important that you allow these experiences to build **confidence** in you as a person. **Confidence** is that feeling you have when you aren't afraid to be the one to take the last shot in the big game.

Confidence is the feeling you get when it's time to accomplish a huge task or achieve a goal and you step right up to the plate.

It is also extremely important that you never confuse being confident with being "cocky". Being "cocky" means that if you happen to make that winning basket during a huge basketball game or finish that hard assignment, that after doing so, you run over and rub it in the faces of the other players or students in the class.

Being "cocky" means that you don't think you have to practice as hard as everyone and that you don't think anyone could ever help you to become even better. Instead, believe in yourself but be respectful to others when you happen to achieve greatness.

Some people will tell you that success means that you have to be the best at whatever it is that you are doing. Some people will tell you that in order to become successful, you must win every game you play in.

But what those people would be forgetting to tell you is that if you are able to improve at the skill you are practicing in class even a little bit, or stand up to a challenge that was once too scary to face, that those moments are also moments of accomplishing success!

And surprisingly, success can even come in the form of how often you treat others the way you would like to be treated. This means that you can be successful at being a friend or classmate. Success is bigger than a test grade in class or winning a game. It is tied to everything we do!

It is important to remember that success doesn't include comparing yourself to anybody else. As long as you are truly giving an assignment or an activity 100% effort, you will find an opportunity to become successful. Success is a life long journey that us adults know is in your future.

Lastly, make your family proud and give people a reason to say, "I want my child or the other students to be like him or her". And for us teachers and parents, if our students can see the importance of caring more than we do, that is all we can ask for when it comes to finding success in the children we love so much!

CHAPTER 4

Write where you are

If we are to be completely honest and realistic with ourselves about the potential for accomplishing any of these dreams of ours, we have to have a system for keeping the thoughts and ideas at the forefront of our thinking.

What I mean by this is that throughout any given day we face thousands of scenarios, make hundreds of choices and because of those factors, prioritizing tasks and plans that we hope to accomplish can be difficult at times. This is usually referred to as putting "things" on the back burner. Additionally for many of us who haven't found a way to keep track of staying focused on our goals, we call it *procrastination.*

Therefore, this chapter suggests exactly what it implies, "write where you are". In order to maintain a consistent approach and maximize your time and efforts, recording your steps, charting your growth, keeping your goals visually accessible and most importantly, reminding yourself that "no, it is not too late" will increase your efforts. Knowing what's happening and remembering to reflect on the process daily will elevate your motivation to pursue that goal.

It is important to remind yourself of the many goals that you are capable of accomplishing. But revisiting these aspirations as the window of opportunity establishes itself only serves as the first step to making these changes a reality. So in order to secure the potential, it will take more than just simply writing down what it is you want to achieve. You will eventually have to take action.

Rather than just writing down ideas and thoughts on a sticky note, or leaving yourself a text-message to remind yourself of these plans, find a way with your own preference, to log the steps that you know or have learned are necessary to get you to where you want to be. Then, be sure to record or keep track of what action you have taken towards successfully achieving even a small amount of progress that will lead you closer to reaching that next level.

This record of necessary steps or the process of keeping your plan updated will also serve as a reminder as to what you have and have yet to do along the journey of maximizing the new opportunity. For example, because of the millions of thoughts and decisions that we have to make every day, sometimes we can forget if we have tried solving a problem with a specific strategy. It may slip our minds, similarly to remembering if we took the chicken out of the freezer yet for dinner. Therefore, we can easily forget at times whether or not we have attempted to inch closer to that dream, or if we have unintentionally taken a step back, with having tried one possible solution.

By remembering what you have already tried that either worked or what would be considered a failed attempt and a learning experience, guess what you are also saving? Time! It is essential to write down your goals and to keep track of the actions you are taking to achieve them. But if you want to be someone like a doctor or engineer, don't just write down those nouns on a sheet of paper. **Elaborate** and **generate** a list of traits those people have. **Identify** how they became who they are and do it. Use the lessons learned from previous attempts, remain focused and stay encouraged throughout the process. Write your journey on paper in your "Goals and Dreams Journal" to keep active and maintain the necessary mindset that it takes to continue on the path of being prepared. By doing so you will become one step closer to achieving success when that window of opportunity opens.

CHAPTER 5

Window of opportunity

When you are unsure about the direction your life is taking, **examine** your situation a little closer. When you are confused about something, the world can seem like a much larger and complicated place. By failing to learn and apply the life-changing lessons that your experiences have the power in teaching you, growing and making the most out of life isn't an easy, comfortable process. But these findings should extend your curiosity instead of causing you to stop **persisting**.

I would argue that the majority of people in our world deal with the ups and downs of emotionally readjusting their outlook on life. Sometimes, the help you need to get on track or back on the path to a successful future doesn't come in the obvious package marked, "The Guide to Figuring Out Your Life". But in some cases, it does.

Take for instance someone who wakes up in their home one morning and to their surprise, smoke has filled their entire house. Immediately, this person would assume that they are in some type of danger. How much danger and how much panic they should exhibit are relative to the person's preparation for such an emergency.

Once it becomes clear that A, they have time to figure out the source of the smoke, and B, they more than likely will be able to save their home from burning to the ground, the person then has choices to make. But now for instance, let's assume the worst within this unwanted scenario. Instead of having time to figure out how serious of an issue this smoke has caused, let us pretend that this person wakes up to a fire that is blazing and growing at a rapid rate.

In this case, the individual would absolutely be at a panic, to find themselves in need of the most immediate and effective support. So, to their rescue comes a helicopter. Not just any helicopter but one that is specifically used to rescue individuals and families from scenarios like this one, from a burning home.

What does the person do next? They get to the *window* and reach out to the ladder that is stationary, and pressed firmly against the side of the house. With the proper and necessary equipment, a rescue worker meets the man or woman who is in dire need of an emergency evacuation, wraps the harness around them and subsequently lifts them off to safety.

In this case, the person who was just rescued will have a second chance at life. And after the damages are repaired and the home is either replaced or rebuilt, the individual who was saved will have an opportunity to not only get their life back together, but they will also have a much greater appreciation for what it means to live.

Now assume for a second that once awaken by that blazing fire and moments before choosing to reach out of that window to be saved, that instead, that individual denied the assistance of the emergency helicopter unit, closed the window and accepted the fate of crumbling down in a blaze of smoke and fire with their home and their worldly possessions.

Does this sound crazy? To deny the obvious, lifesaving help of the rescue unit? Well, when people deny reaching for windows of opportunity that can launch their dreams and allow them to be successful in life by finding success in their goals and aspirations, those same people might as well close that window, inhale the smoke and give up on maximizing their potential in life.

When that individual in the burning house woke up that morning, and they heard and saw the help being offered by the rescue unit, they knew, that it wasn't too late to make it out alive and to see another beautiful day. But it is what you do when you the opportunity presents itself that matters most. Are you going to crumble in fear and uncertainty or will you fight for what you want, and make the most out of your new chances with life?

CHAPTER 6

Reshaping success

Success is not a one size fits all type of concept. This is where being able to **integrate** the failed attempts with new ideas that we get from other experiences comes in handy.

I think it is safe to assume that we have all experienced several examples that fit this suggested experience. Thinking back to the first time I tried making pancakes, I immediately remembered how difficult and disastrous that morning had been. Sure, many people can read the directions and assume that they have measured the ingredients accurately enough to successfully feed themselves and those waiting for you to finish cooking.

But like anything in life that you try for the first time, just like those sloppy, burnt, watery pancakes, the failed attempt allowed me to learn how to improve the process for the next time. Through what many refer to as trial and error, I was able to correct the mistakes, by turning the heat down, accurately mixing the appropriate amount of mix and water to not only make some delicious pancakes, but to prove to myself that success comes to those who aren't afraid to fail. Had I scratched the idea of trying to cook pancakes, I would now have a limited mindset in regards to finding the success out of failure.

The success comes once we stop worrying about how well we think other kids or other people are doing. It might take you a second or third time to try to do the same task or accomplish the same goal. When you don't give up and find the courage to keep working on yourself, that is where success happens. Keep in mind where you start from and how far you have come along while you **construct** your vision for achieving goals that will eventually happen right before your eyes.

The time when I was figuring out the best way for kids to improve their ability at reshaping what success meant to them, had also been around the same time when I met this one student. I had to rub my eyes because of how much he resembled myself. I jokingly went home after the first day of school that year and told my friends that I knew for a fact that I had yet to have a child, but that one kid at my job seemed to resemble my own blood-line more than my own relatives did.

Known as one of the most impulsive and violent students in the building, I immediately knew that I had to find a way to harness his energy. Relationships have been a common theme within my classroom and school community that year. So, naturally I thought, the more I know about a child and his or her family, the more of a handle I could have on their behaviors and on getting them to maximize their effort to focus and concentrate on a successful school year.

This held some truths throughout the year but again, building authentic relationships with students who have had difficult and challenging upbringings, finding it hard to trust strangers or the adults known as "teachers" wasn't an easy task to manage.

Take for instance this one classroom where my *twin* promoted from. The class that this young man had come from a year ago had been so poorly managed and improperly configured that the initial teacher quit after only two weeks of school. The same class, where this young man was a member of would find itself under the reigns of five different teachers in the course of ten months, due to overwhelmingly challenging behaviors ranging from fighting, oppositional defiance, swearing and even physically attacking one of the teachers. So, inconsistent adult supervision and random lesson planning, underserved a mission of closing the space that the achievement gap had created, leaving no chance at making any improvement for those thirty-one students the year prior.

For reasons that I didn't understand, I decided to grow my hair out that school year. After about a year of not cutting the top of my hair, it grew into a Mohawk like shape, where keeping the sides groomed and faded turned it into a stylish, hip new look. At the same time, the professional football player Odell Beckham Jr. was performing as an NFL superstar and coincidently enough, his hair style, that mine closely resembled, became a household trend.

I naturally connected with the young men in my classes as a school teacher for several reasons, some more obvious at times than others. However, during this pivotal time in popular culture, the boys in my classroom identified with me because of how similar this superstar athlete and I's hairstyles were. So, on occasion I would see the boys coming in weekend after weekend with their hair a little longer on the top and twisted as they were preoccupied with twirling their fingers in their hair almost as if to stretch it and style it like Odell Beckham Jr's or…mine.

Behavior trackers where you know…teachers check in with kids who aren't doing that great weren't working for this young man in the beginning of the year. He was still fighting other kids and getting kicked out of class. So almost in desperation, I offered to cut his hair and style it like mine if he could record one day without being aggressive and disruptive in class. After he managed to behave ideally for one day, he came to me the very next day and asked me when I was going to cut it. To keep my promise I asked him if he thought one day of behaving was easy to do. Eventually, I convinced him that if he could behave appropriately and complete most of his work for one whole month, that I would cut his hair and "hook him up".

Needless to say, I had cut his hair four times that year, extending the amount of time he had to perform to the best of his ability along with behaving appropriately. His success was reshaped by a very non-traditional way, but it worked for him. During his yearly meeting with all of his teachers, principal and his mom, where we all met twice a year to update his learning goals, his mother couldn't hold back her tears and we read his data report on the growth that he made that no one said was possible as a reading and math student. More importantly to mention, he went from being sent out of class one hundred and seven times last years to being sent out ten times that entire year. That, was perhaps the miracle that happens once in an entire teaching career, and I was fortunate enough to be a part of it for him.

When I asked him how he felt about school he said to me that, **"You were kind of like a father to me and not having a father at all, having one at school was...ugh...it was cool man. I felt great this year because I used to be off task and get in to a lot of trouble but I did a lot better this year. And I didn't get a lot of suspensions like I did last year. I didn't know how to be successful and I didn't know what being successful looked like until now"**.

If you learned anything from this example it may be that success is what you make it. It comes in even more ways than decreasing the number of negative phone calls home you receive or when you lower the amount of times you're kicked out of class. Surprisingly, success can even come in the form of how often you treat others the way you would like to be treated. This means that you can even be successful at being a friend or family member. Take full advantage of these opportunities at improving your life and the relationships around you. By doing so, you will only be increasing the odds of seeing more outlets for positive experiences.

Oh, and more thing. These goals and dreams you want to accomplish are going to help you out in life. So don't worry about what others think while you are on your way to the top. Do not get into the habit of listening to anything negative people have to say about your efforts or abilities to accomplish goals or tasks. Do not feel the need to **defend** yourself from what these people have to say. Be sure to focus on yourself and on the effort that you give when it comes to believing you can achieve. That way, anything that isn't positive or supportive that people have to say about you, such as "it's too late", won't matter at all.

Had I let what people said about me stop me from believing in myself when I was younger, I wouldn't have been focusing well enough on identifying the windows of opportunity which allowed me to make the most out of myself. If I had let growing up without a father and without any money or new clothes stop me from trying my hardest and caring about my goals and aspirations, my life would have gone down the wrong path.

Instead, listen to your heart when it tells you which way to go in life. By keeping an open mind and focusing on the positive experiences, you'll realize that you have all of the ability you need. All of the tools to become someone and something great right now or very soon are already in your hands. All you have to do if figure out how to use them.

Many kids say things like, "I can't do it!" or "I don't have the **skills**". At some point, we all say things like that. It is because for a moment, we forget to believe in ourselves. When things get hard or scary, feeling like quitting and backing away from something hard is what we think to do. Instead of feeling that way, know that somebody out there who cares about you more than they care about anything in the world, believes that you can do whatever you put your mind to when the time is right. **Determine** the necessary steps and figure out what you already know in order to get started on pursuing your dreams.

CHAPTER 7

We were kids once, too!

Sometimes, what your school or parents forget to tell you is that your teachers, you know the old guy or the old lady who tries to get you to finish all of that work every day, who tells you to spit the gum out, or put the comic book away during writing block, was once a kid themselves.

It's true! Ask them. So what teachers have been through and what we have experienced should give you enough proof that we kind of know what we are talking about when we tell you that "you" can do "it". The tricky part for teachers is getting all of our students to believe in themselves.

Do you think that teachers and other adults live life without ever doubting themselves or fearing something? Trust me when I tell you that the first thing I thought when I decided to write this book was that, "it is going to be too hard, no one is going to like it". Do you think that teachers and other adults don't ever make mistakes? Well, we do.

We find life challenging and just as difficult as you do and sometimes, much more challenging. We also make plenty of wrong choices that we feel will never be corrected. If you don't believe in your own success, chances are, those mistakes will stick around longer than they have to.

But what we learned when we finally became grown-ups was that as long as you don't quit or give up on yourself and keep trying, that eventually you can achieve!

Adults have already failed plenty of science and

social studies tests, forgotten to hand in math homework, missed the winning shot to win the game and spilled all of their lunch on their pants in school. But overtime, we have also figured out that everything always ends up okay.

Something that may seems like a big deal to you now, like being called a name or being made fun of for getting a bad score on a test, always ends with a happy ending when *you* believe in *you*. So eventually, you will learn to ignore what other students or kids say about you. Never allow the negative comments or hurtful words of others trouble you because it only escalates and turns into bigger problems. Although, there are times when you are left with a limited number of choices, try your best to make positive decisions.

But as a young person, it is important to have some context and perspective on your obstacles that exist or that do not exist, which have the potential of hindering or stopping your success.

Take for example the community where I have worked for the last three years. Overwhelmed with drugs, violence and a lack of resources necessary to ensure the safety and success for thousands of elementary and middle school students, my first interaction ever, with one particular female student was life-changing. I had heard of the rumors of how frequently children fought one another and how often a fatal shooting took place in the area where my school was located but to see something first hand is completely different than hearing about it on the news or from a colleague.

Upon arriving to work on the second morning of the 2015-2016 school year, I had approached the last stop light before making a left turn and entering the private parking area for the employees at my school. It was no later than 7:02 a.m. when I spotted who seemed to be a very friendly and responsible ten or eleven-year old girl walking her younger brother across the street. He appeared to be about four or five years old and they were both wearing the uniform indicating that they attended my school.

Of course as a classroom teacher, you never

remember the faces of every student in the building, especially from only being in the building for one day. There are hundreds of task that you have to consider and tons of procedures that you need to familiarize yourself with in order to be effective and proficient with the job at hand. So I didn't feel guilty for not recognizing the young lady and who I assumed to be her little brother.

As the light turned green, signaling my time to take the turn, out of the corner of my eye I noticed two boys about nine and ten years old themselves, wearing different color school uniforms. Before I was able to take another breath, one of the boys ran behind the friendly older sister and her brother, snatched her bag from her and tried to run away.

I immediately viewed this as inappropriate behavior and thought to take action. Before I could pull over and park, the girl let go of the little boy's hand, caught up to the kid who had stripped the bag from her, knocked him on the side of his head, causing him to violently hit the ground, all before grabbing her bag and brother's hand, to calmly and confidently walk the thirty-feet or so into the main entrance of the school building.

Her action was both heroic and violent at the same time. But her hitting the boy and taking her bag back wasn't the strange part. What was odd about the entire incident was how slow and calm she walked after retrieving her bag, with her back turned to both of the boys who had violated her personal space.

Reminding you that this was only my second day of school as the fourth grade teacher in my new building, I had parked, took a few deep breaths and entered my classroom for only the second time for the 2015-2016 school year. Something deep down inside of me made me walk out into the hallway after setting up for the morning and before I could make it through the threshold of the door, in walked the friendly, smiling, and over protective big sister who had just retrieved her book bag from two bothersome boys.

She would prove to my assistant teacher and I that she would be in need of support in regards to dealing with being bullied and with being aggressive. She was prone to fighting almost every day, either on the way to school or on the way home. I would grow to find out that there were a ton of challenges that she faced both socially and financially, similarly to most of the students and families that attended our school. But something was different about her. She didn't act out or behave defiantly because she didn't think school mattered, or because she didn't care. In fact, she cared a lot, which is why she was willing to risk getting hurt and why she was willing to fight in order to receive her education and make it to class each and every morning.

Having her as a student showed me a different side of teaching. It showed me that most kids who are influenced to care about their education, and who someone believes in, remain hungry for a successful future. But every situation is not as dramatic as such. You might not be able to see it right away, but in time, those kids who made you feel bad on the inside, the kids who wanted to fight you or who laughed when you forgot the answer to a few quiz questions will most likely become your best friends.

And if for some reason that doesn't happen, you will move on to only find new friends. Eventually, it will become clear to you, maybe years later that those same kids may find themselves feeling sorry for having mistreated you when you were all kids. They just simply didn't have the right mindset or skills to be successful as a friend to someone.

So the sooner you realize that your teachers and other adults have been in your shoes and know how it feels to be a student at your age, the more willing you will be to learn from them and appreciate their efforts.

CHAPTER 8

We believe in you,
but do you believe in you?

So...hopefully by now it is clear that us teachers and adults who care about all of you students and young people so much were once elementary, middle and high school students ourselves. And what that means is that we know what it is like to struggle to believe.

We know exactly what it feels like to sit in class and have to learn about something that may not seem too interesting right away. We know exactly why all of a sudden, you ask to use the bathroom when you either see or hear your best friend from another class head in that direction.

So believe us when we tell you that we know how smart and creative you all can be when you put your minds to it. Instead of finding excuses for why you don't have the **confidence** in yourself, know that as soon as you make the choice to try, trying becomes a habit. Take for example one student from my past teaching experience.

One day a few years ago I had sat down with one of my favorite students. Those moments of being able to converse without direct instruction are always a fun time. I had never known how to relate to each individual struggle or how to understand where each child was coming from in regards to how they viewed themselves as a student, a son or as a daughter. Each scholar in my classroom had a unique story and each experience was always worth hearing.

Talking to one of my fourth graders at the end of the

school year a few years ago had been a very fascinating experience. She came to my class in August of 2014 with the excitement and energy that you would love to see in every child in America. But what I immediately found out about her is that she was going to teach me, way more than what I was going to instill in her as a learner.

Yes…was the first word she said to me when I asked her to tell me about her year in the fourth grade.

"It was fun, having to learn more of what I had learned in third grade and to be in Yale (the name of our classroom) and to have you, Mr. Mourning as my teacher."

I asked her about how hard she thought everything was for her after having gone to summer school the year before, where I had had the pleasure of teaching her for a full month of additional instruction.

She responded by telling me that fourth grade was hard because there were things that she couldn't do but that she learned how to do them by paying attention. She continued to explain how she was confused as to why the teachers were always redirecting her and that she thought we didn't like her until she went home one afternoon and her mom told her that I had called her to explain how proud I had been that she worked through being upset as she often became emotional with challenging activities and tasks.

The most difficult scenario with this one student was breaking down her barriers that she obviously learned to use to avoid tasks and to get out of doing work that would push her to her limits. I could only imagine what it would have been like to be asked to read grade level texts and to complete written assignments designed for students equipped with the skills that she lacked. I clearly had to differentiate and scaffold tasks and activities for this particular student but what is more important in this case was her willingness to continue trying once her frustration and self-doubting episodes would pass.

She grew to love her classmates and she learned that education was not just something that adults talked about. But instead she learned that if she believed in herself long enough that she could accomplish most of what we asked of her. It is safe to say that though she will continue to be challenged throughout her formal educational journey, she will at least know the importance of giving it her best shot, no matter what obstacles are in front of her.

For those of you who are afraid of trying because you aren't sure if you will be able to make other people around you proud, remember that you don't have to prove yourself to anyone. Instead of worrying about proving people wrong who may not believe in you, focus more on proving yourself right.

The goals and things you want to accomplish are going to help you out in life, so don't worry about what others think while you are on your way to the top. Do not get into the habit of listening to anything negative people have to say about your efforts or abilities to accomplish goals or task.

Be sure to focus on yourself and on the effort that you give when it comes to believing you can achieve.

That way, anything that isn't positive or supportive that people have to say about you won't matter at all.

Had I let what kids said about me stop me from believing in myself when I was younger, I would have never been able to make anything out of myself.

If I had let growing up without a father and without fresh new clothes stop me from trying my hardest and caring about my school work, my life would have gone down the *wrong* path. Instead, listen to adults when they tell you they want to *help* you and that regardless of what your life is like now, you have all of the ability you need.

Let's stop for a second and imagine this...Pretend that you fall overboard off of a huge boat in the middle of an ocean. In that instance, huge waves would come crashing down on you, making it hard to survive. But the waves aren't the only thing that can harm you. There are also sharks! Big ones, too! But if someone threw over a life raft to save you, what would you do?

If you ignore your teachers and adults and instead disrespect the people who care about you, and don't take us serious when we tell you that you can "do it", it is the same as ignoring the life raft that was thrown overboard to save your life.

Instead of being pulled up to safety, you would be left stranded in the ocean with those life threatening waves, oh and the sharks. Can't forget about the sharks. Instead of accepting the support and making "trying your hardest" a new habit, you would be letting yourself sink deeper and deeper into the ocean, never reaching land again.

The same way those people using that life raft would be trained to properly bring you to safety is the same way your teachers are trained in caring for you.

Your teachers are trained to make sure you are ready for the challenges of hard school work. Your parents and other adults are experienced enough to point you in the right direction during a challenging time in your life. They are also trained to make sure that when you get to the next grade or turn another year older, that you are confident in yourselves. We are trained to make sure that you believe that the life raft can save you, to ensure that you can be successful at whatever it is that you have to do, pulling you out of the dangerous waters and on to safe, dry land.

But that isn't enough! The point of this book is to show you that of course we care about you and that we believe in you. However, you have to believe in yourself even more than we do and **interpret** these **skills** in a way that you can use them throughout your life and **recall** them when necessary.

How many of you have ever said, "I can't do it". At some point, we all say things like that. It is because for a moment, we forget to believe in ourselves. It is because, in those true moments of feeling **inadequate**, we feel that we can **justify** or explain giving up on ourselves.

When things get hard or scary, feeling like quitting and backing away from something hard is what we think to do. It's natural...I get it. But instead of feeling that way, know that somebody out there who cares about you more than they care about anything in the world, believes that you can do whatever you put your mind to.

Unfortunately, you can only make it so far in life before you run out of luck. Those people who make it the furthest in life like Lebron James, Stephen Curry, and Nicki Minaj, only make it to the top because they never give up believing in themselves more than other people believe in them.

CHAPTER 9

Learn to love something

This chapter is about exactly what it says. I am challenging you to "learn to love" school because...well...let's be honest...you have to go! So you might as well enjoy the seven or eight hours that you are in the building instead of waiting to go home or feeling negatively towards your opportunities to get better at life.

As it so happens, when I decided to write this book

for young people to understand their role in their journey to success, I had mentioned my idea out loud. In passing, one of my most entertaining students heard me and this is what he brought to my attention...

"I overheard Mr. Mourning explaining that he wanted to write a second book and that he wanted us kids to all have a say in what it was going to be about. But see, I had to tell my man Mr. Mourning that if he was going to write a book, that I could write my own section in it.

He said we couldn't use our real names but all you need to know is that I'm the man. We have chants and cheers that our entire school uses and we compete in a classroom chant shout off every Wednesday Morning. During the chants, it mean a lot to me that our class wins. The class that uses the most positive lyrics and who shows pride in doing well in academic achievement usually wins. I'm loud during the chants and I lead them. But sometimes, I'm loud when I'm not supposed to be. Every time Mr. Mourning sees my mother he tells her that I

have so much potential but I already know that. I usually get in trouble for talking and being out of my seat and not because I want to get in trouble but because being in our class is too exciting to stay in one spot all day.

I kind of don't understand why we always get in trouble for standing up but like, I know that they want us to listen and not get in trouble so I try my hardest to follow the rules.

One thing that I still don't understand is why the school has those crazy behavior rules or like, behavior policy things. And recess is short. And the food-- The food is mainly nasty and sometimes I get so hungry by 1:30 that it don't even matter and I eat it anyway. I also disagree with the time of specials because it's right in the morning and then we have to sit down and learn for the whole rest of the day. And also the after-care program doesn't have sports for us and they should because the boys in aftercare are very active and like to play football, basketball and other types of sports but they don't have that.

But one thing that I love are the chants and cheer off competition...and it is mainly the reason why I do my best in school...at least for now".

I'm not too sure if you would understand how intuitive or smart that young man is who just typed up his own section. He is highly capable of performing above average or even at an advanced level on certain formal academic assessments. But what is the most interesting about this young man is that despite his upbringing and his fatherless household, he has identified on his own, what he does not want to become when he is an adult.

He reminds me so much of myself in the sense that he has a single, independent mother, a caring grandfather and an amazing ability to perform in front of large crowds, bringing them to their feet with participation. I wouldn't be exaggerating by saying that if I could do school all over again, that I would love to be that kid. He learned how to love something and as he said, for now...it works for him.

You might as well find a way to be the best at

something in the building. If you want to be great at something, whether it's cheerleading, or soccer, or football or singing or dancing or any of the amazing things our world provides us chances to do, you have to be willing to try harder than other people. And sometimes, you will have to do things that you *don't want to do* or that you *don't understand right away.*

You will have to be able to do things that other kids aren't willing to try. For example, if you want to be the best dancer, you may have to be able to perform in front of a thousand people at some point. Some of your friends who also think that they are great dancers might not have the **confidence** to do this.

And moments like this is what separates kids who are good at something from kids who are great! You have to be willing to do things that others aren't ready for in order to be the best at what you love.

If you learn to understand the importance of practicing a skill, and if you ever get to the point where practicing hard on something is what you look forward to, just imagine how great you can become when you allow this love for getting better to become habit and routine.

Without practicing a skill, whether it's basketball or reading, you cannot get any better at it. If you have ever wanted to be like those super stars on T.V, do know that they don't argue with their teammates when they are asked to try harder or to stay longer to put in more effort.

This extra effort at *loving to learn* is what it takes in order to become the absolute best at anything. And being someone that people can rely on and knowing that you can rely on yourself is powerful.

CHAPTER 10

The power of being accountable

Being accountable means more than just having the ability to allow family members, friends, and classmates to be able to count on you. Having **accountability** means that when someone needs help, you find the time and energy to be there for them. Thinking about the best way to communicate this concept of accountability to young people, I immediately think back to maybe…three or four years ago when I sat down with a young lady who became known as my prime example for being a responsible young person.

When sitting down at lunch to talk to her some years back, this is what she had said…

"Being the oldest girl (ten years old) in my house is like being a mom because I always have to baby sit them, sometimes. And sometimes my aunt is there to watch us all but when I usually have to watch them they are monsters, always attacking me and never letting me sleep. And then sometimes… when I usually watch them it is when my mom goes out. I'm done".

At the time when I realized that this girl was a very responsible and mature ten-year old, I had no idea of the responsibilities that were put on her plate. So naturally, without having a strong relationship with this student it caused me to make assumptions that would soon be changed and clarified as the year went on. I couldn't understand as to why at ten years old, this young lady was so angry and frustrated on a daily basis. Sometimes, she would be completely disconnected from learning and from interacting with her peers from the moment she sat down to eat breakfast. I slowly started to see her participation wither away and reduce itself to sleeping for half of the class. Her energy was extremely low, which caused her to fall behind with reading and with learning new math concepts that the fourth grade required.

I asked the student, "what was the turning point from not liking school and feeling like never wanting to be here, to wanting to be in class participating and doing your best, eventually becoming one of the leaders in our classroom, although her attitude persisted.

"When you told us to get our act together, that is one time when I changed my attitude."

But what did that really mean to her? "Get your act together?"

"My mom also tells me that school is important but she doesn't seem to care as much as you do about me and that's crazy to me because I don't even know you like I know my mother".

I went on to ask her what she feels like when she is

with us at school compared to being at home where she often has to baby sit her four younger siblings, feeling at times as if she is a ten year old mother. She went on to say...

"well like, I don't live with you guys and you make me mad when you tell me to do things over and over until I get it right. That's not right Mr. Mourning, but I get it and now I know why you always make me try my hardest. If I learn something then I can become somebody and that's what y'all want from me".

Being a classroom teacher has never been so difficult as it has been working for the past few years in "turn-around" charter schools in the heart of Washington, D.C. But at the same time, where violence and poverty have been synonymous for years, life as a teacher has never been so rewarding.

I often have to reflect behind closed doors as to why on earth I would endure such frustration and challenging relationships with parents and adults who are themselves, products of failed educational opportunities and financial hardship. I have concluded that it is because of these experiences and chances to see growth happen right in front of my eyes, that gives me the strength to continue my journey to service those that I have grown to love and appreciate the most. The most responsible and accountable young people learn from both committed teachers and their own challenging life experiences.

Accountability also means, when it is your responsibility to complete a task or a class assignment, that you make sure you get it done to the best of your ability.

People can be accountable for something as simple as being asked to baby sit. Instead of staying out at the ball park for longer than they choose to, they come right home and take care of their responsibility.

Students can be accountable by borrowing supplies in a classroom and placing them exactly where everyone else expects to find them. This is also known at times as having **integrity**. Sound familiar?

But do not be fooled. We are experts and can tell if you are actually learning to care about your education as much as we need you to. And...we can tell if you are faking it. Imagine if Stephen Curry pretended to go practice all of those extra three-point shots and never really went onto the court to get better. If he chose to fake it and pretend to practice he would only be hurting himself.

Therefore, when teachers or adults ask you to be *accountable* it means to actually put in the effort and do what you need to do in order to get better.

Doing what your teachers and parents asks you to do, will only help you to achieve success. Do not pretend to shoot those three pointers or pretend to read because you won't improve. Actually do the work! Actually practice those extra math questions. Because if you pretend, or fake it, you will never be the best that you can be.

Make doing the right thing a habit because being accountable and caring will end up sticking with you forever. This will allow you to continue becoming the best and eventually, you will care way more than us teachers and parents ever have.

And for my students and young people who have used this phrase before, "It wasn't even me!"...Again, understand that teachers and parents are experts. Chances are, whatever your teacher or guardian said you did, you did do and here is what you should do next. Instead of arguing or pouting about it, accept the redirection.

Adults only stop to point out what you are doing wrong in order to get you back on track so that you can continue learning how to get better at reading, writing, math or at being the best version of yourself that you can be.

Adults only spend the time getting you back on task because they care about you more than anything in the world. Also, they know that if you try your hardest you can be successful at anything you put your mind to.

The same goes for when teachers have to raise their voices or use a stronger tone. We are never angry with *you* or upset at *you*. We never think for a second that you are "bad kids". Sometimes, good kids just make poor choices.

So instead, think of us raising our voices or redirecting you as if to say, "we know how amazing you are when you try your hardest and we expect that from you all of the time". If we as adults didn't raise our voices, it would in fact mean that we *do not care*. And that you know is already not the case...we care a whole lot!

CHAPTER 11

Follow my lead

Accountability also means that you are capable of doing the right thing when no one is watching. This example is also used to describe what it means to be a *leader.* By doing so, it will become a habit of yours to lead, later in life.

For example, if you see trash in the hallways of your school, or dirty dishes in the sink at home and choose not to pick it up or decide not to wash them because no one is there in the hallway or in the kitchen with you, chances are, you won't care to take care of it when you *are* with someone.

Here is where students take their ability to believe in themselves with a little **accountability** and turn into a teacher's favorite word, "leaders".

What it means to lead is that you can be trusted by adults and classmates to not only do what is right, but to do it exceptionally well. Leaders are often identified showing, rather than telling. Leading, is often done by example and not by "saying" you are going to do something the right way. Leading can also be done in another way.

No matter what people tell you, it is okay to remove yourself from crowds of kids or students who act inappropriately at times. You know, the crowd of kids at recess, lunch time or after school that causes trouble. This is often done by the group or individual who seems not to care about school as much as we all know we should. In a final attempt to influence students to follow your lead, you can attempt to be a peer **mediator**, where you focus on the problem and not the behaviors that are being displayed by your friends or classmates. You can try asking kids who don't get along to tell each other how being treated poorly makes them both feel in attempts to unite kids who may actually grow to be great friends in the future. But don't cause yourself more problems if kids don't seem to respond to your positive approach in a reasonable way or in a reasonable amount of time.

Being able to surround yourself with other respectful and caring young people will make your life a whole lot easier when you get older. But don't take my word for it. Write down a list of your current friends and next to their name, jot down if they are kind, caring, respectful, honest and whether or not they stay out of trouble. You might be surprised as to what you write down. But maybe after sharing this book with them, and after a few weeks of new and positive experiences, you'll be able to **revise** your list.

But the most important step of knowing how to be a leader and how to know what you should be acting like is by being able to identify the characteristics on your own. Take for example a young scholar athlete who I have had the privilege of teaching throughout the past seven years…She adds to this concepts beautifully.

"Well, my brother is a really good football player but that don't even matter if you don't have the best grades. But yeah…that makes me proud and that makes me wanna be like him…get the best grades and be a really good tennis player. Mr. Mourning, I don't know how you did it. I don't know how you kept coming back to work when the kids would act crazy and talk and be rude".

Man, I love my job but this young lady showed me yet, another side of education. She proved that kids can teach adults just as much and in some cases, way more than we can teach them. She reminded me that not all troubled, at-risk students were from the same backgrounds. She showed me that although she attended our "substantially deficient academic community", that she was in fact a high performing student with goals and dreams that will eventually take her further than any privileged suburban female student-athlete.

I chose to ask her why she likes school, making the assumption that she did based on how well she behaved and how well she performs and her response was fitting.

"I like school because it gives me an education and it allows me to express myself. I can achieve my dream which is being a professional tennis player. I'm gonna make that happen by following my brother's footsteps and never giving up trying to achieve it. And I could be higher than Serena Williams. I could be successful and change people by helping them make their dreams come true and making my family happy".

It is no surprise to me why some students do better than others when opportunities in their late teens arise. It is clear that this young lady has had a foundation that included caring adults, successful siblings, great teachers, and college oriented goals outlined for her either directly or indirectly in her own home and within her life outside of class. But more importantly, she had showed me that she cared about her own future more than adults did for her. I can't wait to see how far she makes it because after a year of knowing this one student, I know that deep down inside, it isn't a matter of if, but simply a matter of when, that she will accomplish anything and everything that she puts her mind to.

And do understands this final piece of advice about **leadership**. Leaders often grow up to stick together. Those that decide on making the appropriate choices in school, or at a sports practice and even at home usually are the most successful grown-ups when the time comes for them to become an adult.

Fortunately, because you haven't become adults just yet, you still have time to not only become that young role model for your school or **community**, but you also *still* have time to allow your brain to make choosing the best option during your journey from childhood to adulthood, a true habit!

Regardless of if you want to have the attention of other classmates or adults, the reality of our world is that you can't escape this spotlight. No matter if you choose to be an active leader or not, people such as friends, teammates and especially teachers and parents, are aware of the choices you make or choose not to make. So in the case of being upset by something or someone, your reactions are being recorded, whether you want them to be noticed or not. Therefore, never let a minor problem in your life such as spilling juice on your shirt, or not getting a turn during a game or competition at school or at home **escalate** and ruin **major** moments throughout your day.

Nothing that you attempt in life goes unseen. So in the case of caring more than "us", care to been seen leading in the right direction.

CHAPTER 12

Improve your life
one day at a time

Being a little better at something than you were yesterday is what caring about yourself more than your teachers and adults do, is all about. You do not have to get 100's on all of your test tomorrow if you have never gotten a 100% on anything ever before.

But taking a test and scoring a 70% the first time, and then getting an 80% the next time shows your teachers and other adults that you do in fact care to improve! Asking a friend if they are doing okay, when the day before you would have ignored that they were crying or sad, shows your teachers and other adults that you do in fact, care!

Showing **empathy** and putting yourself in someone else's shoes is not only a sign of maturity, but it will improve your own life by providing you a chance to appreciate who you are and what opportunities lie ahead for you. Young people who can think this way are the types of students and kids that teachers and adults are going to be more willing to help out when things get confusing or tricky in class or in life.

This does not mean that I am asking you to become a perfect student or perfect young person! No one is perfect and that is absolutely normal. Life is about trying your hardest, making mistakes and getting up again to show yourself what you learned from the experience.

In the case that academic excellence and exceptional behavior is not what you are used to, take pride in knowing that there are caring and loving adults who are now looking up to you. We are now expecting you to be the role models for the younger students in your school and neighborhoods. Which for some of you, it may mean that it's time to get your act together. We are expecting you to believe in yourselves and to **respect** your family, friends and classmates along the way.

So start today in making your life even better than it was yesterday. What are you waiting for? Get out there and volunteer to help someone tomorrow in school. Ask a classmate who you usually never have a chance to speak to if they are having a good day. Stay on task during that math lesson longer than you usually do. Because when you focus on one small part of your life at a time, you have a higher chance at improving your opportunities of being great!

If you are fortunate enough to find success throughout your journey, one day you may find yourself asking a group of students or younger people to learn how to care more than you do. The next step for you is to take all of this in, figure out what can help you and what makes sense to you by **paraphrasing** and taking notes. But move forward with patience and self-discipline. Good Luck and remember that you always have a choice. Make it count towards something awesome!

A Special Thank you...

On a cold October afternoon, my stomach was twisting and turning with anxiety. I was only ten years old and yet, I had been exposed to more opportunities to assume adult like responsibilities than most twenty year olds are given. I was often **responsible** for making sure my two siblings and I at the time made it to school before 7:45 a.m. every morning. I was more often than not, the person checking to make sure that the three of us had clean clothes for the next day and that our homework was done the night before school. And more importantly to mention, I was responsible for keeping us safe.

On that winter-like afternoon back in 1997, I was

living the life of being one of the top youth football players in my town for the past two years. As a young athlete, football was one of the only things in my life that I seemed to have success with. Therefore, the opportunity of achieving my goal of one day becoming a professional football player was what I held onto the most. I was determined and had all of the intentions in the world on keeping that momentum going for myself.

Although I had the potential of being a young super-star in the making, there was one obstacle in the way, which almost prevented me from achieving my goals. Throughout my childhood, my mother didn't have a car. This often caused my siblings and I to miss out on several extracurricular opportunities. From our school to the playing fields, I could remember everything being very far away and out of walking distance.

Missing practices and making excuses for not being able to participate in activities several miles away from my home would have been understandable. But as life would go on, I came to find out that by not allowing obstacles to stop me from maximizing my chances to achieve great things, and by never giving up hope even when things aren't going my way, that at some point a window of opportunity will come along

So on that cold, damp afternoon in October of 1997, as a ten year old football player and big brother, I walked three miles to practice with my youth football team that day. And about one hundred feet from the parking lot, after a forty-five minute hike, I was approached by a car. Driving was the father of a family whose son played on my team and they asked me how long I had been walking. And what I remember telling them was that, I didn't know for sure, but I knew that I didn't want to miss my chance to be the best football player in town that season. As chances had it, I became the kid who one of the football families would consistently pick up and bring home from practice for the next couple of years of our career as youth football players. The Weiss family did what they thought was right and little did they know, making an extra seat in their car for those years of making it to practice on time, saved my life.

From that day on, I saw the power in taking action. I chose to be accountable and to never use excuses for the lack of opportunities to improve my own life. Instead, I realized that by showing effort and trying your hardest to get the job done, that it would always maximize my chances at a positive future.

By identifying open windows of opportunity, it is never too late to find a way out of no way. My mother was only one more stressful afternoon away from pulling me off of that team because of her not knowing how she was going to provide safe and adequate transportation for her first son. She had made it clear that my dreams were important to her but she couldn't handle the stress of wondering if I would make it safely across town each and every day. But perhaps walking, as safe of a route as I knew, I somehow showed my dedication and passion to the world, which changed the trajectory of my life for the better.

Only God knows where I would have ended up had I been limited to living a life without football, without the motivation, the excitement, the discipline and character building opportunities that extracurricular opportunities have the power in providing. So remember, if you have to do a little bit of walking before the ups and downs of that journey show you some promise of why it'll all be worth it, just remember to look both ways.

And in 2009, after completing four years of College, receiving two degrees and participating as a full-scholarship athlete, I thank those who stopped along the road to success and who offered me a ride. Life...what a ride it will be.

Glossary

Key terms to Caring More Than Us:

Accountability-the state or quality of being accountable.
Example: There is no one to complain to about the problem because there is no accountability in that department.

Analyze-to separate into parts for close study; examine and explain.
Example: If we analyze the problem, perhaps we can solve it.

Citizen-a person who is a member of a country either because of being born there or being declared a member by law.
Example: As citizens of the town, we can vote in the election for the office of mayor.

Classify-to group or order in classes.
Example: He classified his coin collection according to type and age.

Commitment-a pledge or obligation to fulfill an act or function.
Example: The government has made a commitment to cleaning up the environment.

Community-a particular area where a group of people live.
Example: A new store opened next to the school in my community.

Comprehend-to understand or grasp the meaning of.
Example: Did you comprehend what the teacher said?

Confidence-a sense of trust or faith in a person or thing, or in oneself.
Example: She has confidence in the work I do. He writes with great confidence.

Conscious- done on purpose; deliberate.
Example: Did she make a conscious choice to turn in her work late?

Construct-to build; put together.
Example: They constructed the garage in three days.

Correlates-to arrange, as two sets of data, so as to demonstrate or emphasize their causal, reciprocal, complementary relationship
Example: *The results of the new study do not correlate clearly with the results of the previous experiments.*

Defend-to speak, write, or act in support of.
Example: He defended his beliefs in an article in the newspaper.

Determine-to conclude after studying or watching.
Example: Some scientists have determined the age of the dinosaur teeth.

Elaborate-to add details to something; explain more fully (often followed by "on" or "upon").
Example: Elaborate on your ideas for building a new library.

Empathy-identification with or sharing of another's feelings, situation, or attitudes.
Example: The play didn't interest him as he could not feel empathy with characters having such great wealth and high social status.

Escalate-to increase in intensity, scope, or size.
Example: We will escalate the war against crime. His demands soon escalated.

Examine-to look at closely and carefully.
Example: We examined an insect with a magnifying glass.

Extend-to make longer in size; make last longer.
Example: We extended the ladder so that it would reach the top of the tree. The teacher extended recess by fifteen minutes.

Generate-to bring into being or to produce.
Example: The class had to generate a list of ideas for the school play.

Identify-to figure out or show who someone is or what something is.
Example: The scientist had to identify if the bird was a rare kind of parrot.

Influence-the power or invisible action of a thing or person that causes some kind of effect on another.
Example: Her father plays the drums and had a lot of influence on her decision to play the drums too.

Integrate-to bring together and mix into a whole.
Example: Comic strips integrate two art forms: drawing and writing.

Integrity-a strong sense of honesty; firmness of moral character.
Example: He showed great integrity when he refused to lie for his employer.

Interpret-to decide on or explain the meaning of.
Example: How do you interpret his latest book?

Justify-to show good reasons or cause for.
Example: I justified eating the last piece of pie by saying that it would be thrown away otherwise.

Leadership-ability or skill as a leader.
Example: She showed leadership when asked to take over the meeting.

Major-greater in size or number.
Example: The congressman played a major part in getting the seatbelt laws passed.

Mediator-to act as an intermediary in (a dispute) or bring about (an agreement).
Example: The lawyer was the mediator for two sides when they couldn't come to an agreement.

Minor-less important or serious than others of the same kind.
Example: My problem is a minor one compared to yours.

Paraphrasing-to have restated in somewhat different words.
Example: After paraphrasing the information for me I understood what my mother was referring to.

Patience-the ability to stay calm when there is a delay.
Example: He waited for the bus with patience. Persisting- to continue in a course of action or hold on to a belief in a firm, steady way.

Persisting-to continue in a course of action or hold on to a belief in a firm, steady way.
Example: My mother showed how persisting in refusing to allow me to go was her way of protecting me.

Recall-to bring a past event into the mind; remember.
Example: Do you recall the day we went to the zoo together?

Respect-the state or condition of being thought of with honor or admiration; such admiration itself.
Example: My grandparents enjoy the respect and love of our entire family.

Responsibility-something for which a person is responsible
Example: Cleaning the bathroom is my responsibility. The puppy is your responsibility.

Revise-to correct or edit so as to improve.
Example: I revised my paper before turning it in.

Skills-the power or ability to perform a task well, especially because of training or practice.
Example: After taking this class, her writing skills have improved.

Here is where you can write down your favorite parts to your guide to success OR any advice that you plan on using too make tomorrow a better day!

Here...I'll get you started!

*Always believe in myself no matter what people say about me

_____

_____

_____

_____

_____

_____

_____

_____

_____

_____

_____

_____

_____

_____

_____

_____

_____

_____

_____

ABOUT THE AUTHOR

Glen Leroy Mourning was born on March 26th, 1987 in Danbury, Connecticut. As the oldest of his mother Lillian's five children, Glen was blessed with the opportunity to lead by example where he would become the first of two generations to not only graduate from high school, but to complete a masters degree.

In 2005 Glen earned a Full-Athletic Scholarship to attend the University of Connecticut where he would make the "All Big East Conference Academic Honor roll for two years in a row before graduating and attending Grad School at the University of Bridgeport.

In 2010 Glen finished his master's degree in Elementary Ed. and was named the Student teacher of the year at the University of Bridgeport. Since then, Glen worked alongside of the Nationally renowned Educational contributor Dr. Steve Perry, Star of the CNN Special "Black in America II" and the host of TV One's "Save our Sons".

As a fourth and fifth grade teacher at Capital Preparatory Magnet School in Hartford Connecticut, Glen managed to brilliantly inspire the lives of hundreds of students in his tenure as an educator. At the same time, he was the assistant Varsity football coach at Capital Prep where the team posted an incredible record of 22-2, winning State play-off appearances before stepping down from his role as the defensive backs coach.

For the past three year, Glen has worked in South East Washington D.C as a fourth grade teacher. Next year, Glen will continue working in Elementary Education in Washington, D.C. as he plans on becoming a principal of his own school in the future.

Glen's greatest accomplishments are not those that have occurred on the playing field but rather working for the last seven years to keep his promise to his family. That is; working to become the motivation for those who come from similar circumstances that Glen faced as a young student. His message to those willing to listen is to, "never stop dreaming, even when one comes to an end". For more information about Glen Mourning the author, educator and motivational speaker, visit: www.mourningknows.com